WITHDRAWN

Amphitheatre Publications Ltd.

I wish to express my gratitude to Jeff Bien for his encouragement and the countless hours he devoted to this project.

Some of the poems in this book have appeared in *More Garden Varieties Two* (Mercury Press), 1990, *The Canadian Jewish News,* and *The Lost And Found* (Amphithreatre Publications Ltd.), 1990.

Cover photograph: Natalie Schonfeld
Photo editor: Rafi Aaron
Book design: Marie-José Crête

Canadian Cataloguing in Publication Data
Aaron, Rafi 1959-
A seed in the pockect of their blood
Poetry combined with the works of several photographers.
ISBN 0-9682665-0-9

1. Judaism-Poetry. 2. Landscape photography-Israel.
3. Israel-Pictorial works. I. Title
PS8551.A76S43 1997   C811'.54   C97-900926-X
PR9199.3.A12S43 1997

To order this book or the travelling exhibit comprised of the poems and photographs in
A SEED IN THE POCKET OF THEIR BLOOD

Please contact:
Amphitheatre Publications Ltd.
P.O. Box 43527
Leaside Post Office
Toronto, Ontario
M4G 4G8, Canada

info@amphitheatre.com

Published by Amphitheatre Publications Ltd.
Printed In Hong Kong

Rafi Aaron

A SEED IN THE POCKET OF THEIR BLOOD

Amphitheatre Publications Ltd.

TO REGINE
WHOSE ENTHUSIASM IS CONTAGIOUS —
IT ALMOST MADE ME SMILE!

AS YOU KNOW
IT'S A LONG WAY
FROM MONTREAL
TO N.Y AND
EVEN FURTHER
FROM N.Y TO
MONTREAL.

LOOKING FORWARD
TO WORKING WITH YOU
BEST WISHES FOR HEALTH
+ HAPPINESS

DEC. 1, '99
TORONTO

This book is dedicated to my grandfather

Benjamin Feinstein

in celebration of his 99th year

of spiritual, mental and physical activity.

PART I

PART 2

WHERE i WRITE

it is this moment
i enter the calm of the cove
the sun bows
a red bandanna touches the earth
a gold sash ties
the white robed sky

here i am an explorer
without a flag or a country
all i claim is myself

silently my pen dips
into thought and i glide
leaving a thin blue line

GENESIS

when i wake before you
it is summer on the mountain
the wind asleep
breathes easy with you

i stare into darkness
trees and peaks
crack the black shell
birds speak, the damp earth
cries for a seed
cold air covers my arms
and i wait for you
to rise
with all your warmth—
the sun on this the first day

"AND DAVID MOVED THROUGH A SECRET PASSAGE TO CONQUER THE CITY"

we stand outside these ancient walls
your fingers follow the stream of Shiloah
scraping secrets from a stone tongue
of lime and ore and you are the one, the only one
who knows how the city fell

as you turn towards me
hammers lift and fall the stone cracks
a torch shines on the sweat of one face
and from beyond the wall tapping
loud and louder
the picks swing
the membrane of fine quartz
about to break like a woman's water
rushing into history with a new king

and so David rode into the city
on a white stream
cupped his hands to drink
sentries and their captains died of thirst

now you stand here on the ramparts
not a general but a lover
intimate with Jerusalem's secrets, its scars
you point to the tombs of Absalom and Zechariah
i wait for your touch
knowledge is in your hands

THE DESERT

1 and so you have appeared
   as the bedouin tracker
   placing your hands on stones of fire
   covering your mouth with a white veil
   turning into the desert

   at night you wander my dreams
   i feel the weight of your body
   as you make footprints in the sand

2 the morning a silver dagger
   i turn away but you are there
   in the distance orange and blue
   vapours that sweep over the tracks

   and you speak of slow moving caravans
   swift marauders, a betrothed who fled
   and men buried with treasures

3 it was the khamsin
   that brought you back to my lips
   burning, peeling the skin
   the first drops
   from the water pouch
   soothing healing
   the lips pressed and the water flowed
   like kisses
   soothing and healing

4   in a sandstorm
we watched the desert slash our trail
and so you said, "we exist in a place
where everything perishes
even footprints"

the temperature fell into night
your body could not forget
the heat of the day

5   by a stranger's tent
the coffee is black
as the desert night
i cannot count the stars
or the visions that fell
like beads of sweat
as i waited for you to appear

i listen as our tale is retold
the narrator's hands move
small details bloom from his mouth
and flourish in the silence of the sands

but only the hunters who travelled the plain
will know our vastness
how we survived and others died

and as the brush burns in the fire he speaks
the language of thirst saying
"her beauty was what all men dream of
on the fifth day, when the mouth is cracked
and the throat will no longer swallow"

CAESAREA

we came here like Romans
to retreat from the world
to unclasp our armour
exposing white skin to sun

we lay in the sand
closed our eyes
and were home in the heat
of the bathhouse
the oil poured out of clay jugs
and danced down our spines

we traded coins
commemorating times
in a faraway place
spoke our own language
and felt the empire
on the tip of our tongues

in the shade of palm trees
we watched the wind ribbon sails
sent runners to inform the provinces
our skin had bronzed
we were neither statues nor gods

FLOATING

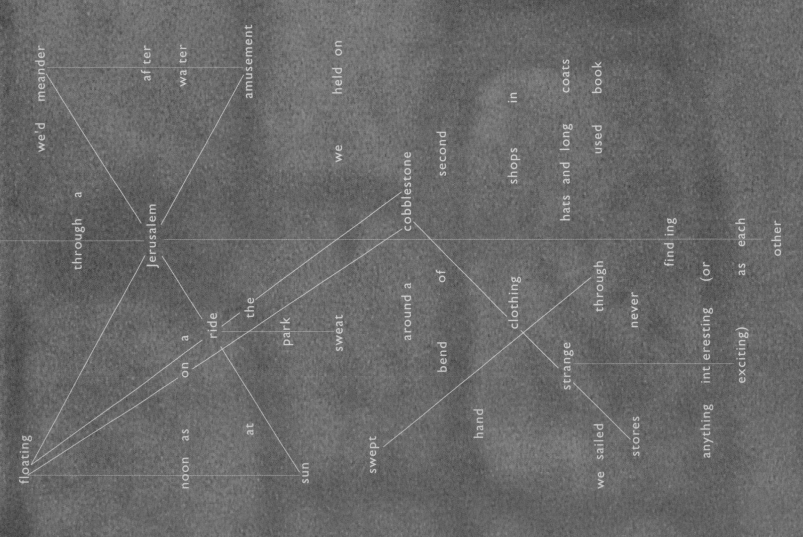

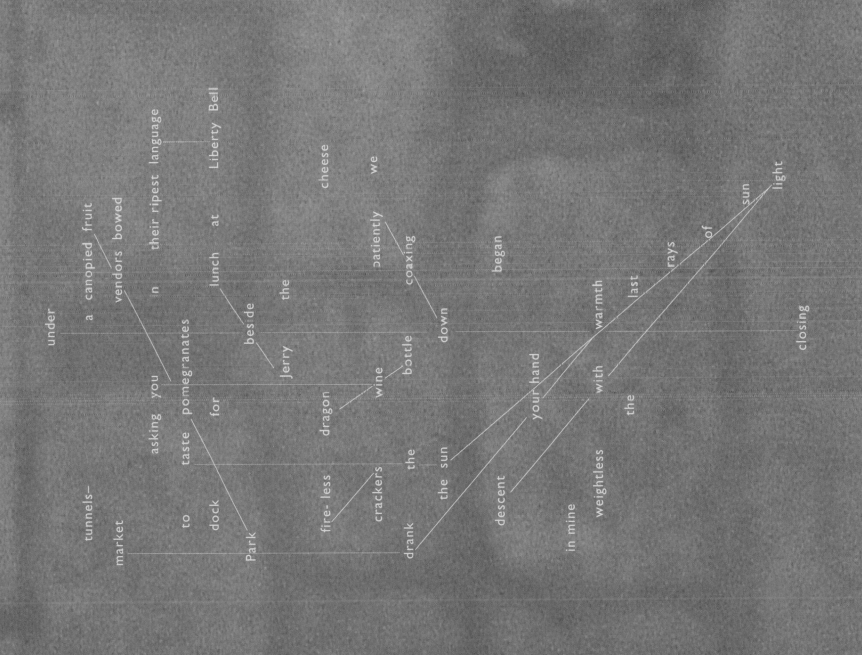

FLOATING (2)

floating we'd meander
through a Jerusalem afternoon
as on a water ride
at the amusement park
sun, sweat, we held on
and were swept around
a cobblestone bend
of second hand clothing shops

in strange hats and long coats
we sailed through used book stores
never finding anything
as interesting (or exciting)
as each other

under tunnels—
a canopied fruit market
vendors bowed asking you
in their ripest language
to taste the pomegranates

dock for lunch
at Liberty Bell Park
beside Jerry the fireless dragon

cheese, crackers, wine
patiently we drank the bottle
coaxing the sun down

descent began
your hand in mine
weightless with warmth
the last rays of sunlight
before closing

REMEMBER THE CASTLE

now i remember the castle
how we climbed all afternoon
entered the stone gates
and took the tower

and you stood there alone
like this mountain
looking over the trade routes
waiting for the caravans to pass

and it was at this spot
where we watched the sands move
without feeling the wind
you raised a staff
on the narrow bridge
between the old and new worlds,
soon kings and thieves
would empty their purses

then wrist on wrist
we pledged to defend
what we had conquered
on this day, and we joined hands
with those who had come
from Jerusalem and Constantinople
as we held this mountain
for one afternoon

IN THIS AMPHITHEATRE

in this amphitheatre
stones have been a silent spectator
an untransmitting scribe
to our secluded meetings in the night

we sat on stone seats unaware
of Romans and architecture
held our breath to the blackened Judean desert
a poor rival for suspended settlement lights
pinpoints on the frustrated blue skyline

whose conquest over the last streaks of sunlight failed
as the late hour grey
floated unevenly
occasionally to submerge in quiet green

and how i sat alone
when you left me
the vanquished desert no longer a mystery
on its empty stage your hair flowed
the settlement lights monopolized the sky
as the need for stars diminished
without your searching hand

to this oasis i brought you
into my long secluded moments
of marvel at man's hands
embedded perfectly into nature's puzzle

now stained in the fog of your features

i have taken all the symbolism
from these symbols
into which you carved your name
and called night
i cannot erase what is enshrined in stone
merely supplement the sullen chapters
with flow of tinted hair

her shivering shoulders from the winter winds
the candle she holds breaks sequence of the stars
and i look onto this night
once again as night

JAFFA

on a porch in Jaffa
a poem can appear
like wind from the sea

this is a place
where people see the past
like the tower clock
telling today's time
with yesterday's parts

and in this restaurant
everyone is an archaeologist
digging into hearts
for signs of life long ago

sipping my coffee i turn to the waiter
ask "what happened to the couple
who met here every day?"
pointing to the pier he says
"it was over there"
but does not know their story

they came before evening
to watch the sun spread
a thin crimson line on the water
and the white caps turn
red and holy
holding the day to darkness

as the wind retreats
i walk down to the market
a young couple
examines what they hold
uncertain if it's tin or gold

PIONEERING

and so we are halutzim
on this barren land
clearing boulders from our field
dragging a dream of orchards
across the dusty earth

the sun burns
water is rationed
the world looks away
but we believe
our hammers will break
the odds and out of the rock
and out of the weed
we will grow

in a darkened field
we summon tired muscles to dance
sing the songs of youth
and with one hand on my heart
the other on a shovel
i recite the manifesto of love

2

THE MODEL FAMILY

i am handed another piece, carefully i squeeze the tweezers

bend over and place the hand-knitted scarf

around my uncle's neck

a house a neighbour lived in

is lifted and lowered to its correct location

gently the grocer's horse is hitched

to a wagon and with the miniature brush

i sweep under the chairs

searching for what the family

has lost or forgotten

and just as another day is closing

the street lamps are lit

the shop doors locked

and the blinds lowered

my relatives head on their way

i glance at those things

they believe existed

but old diaries have contradicted

and quietly i remove them

from the model of their lives

THE PHOTOGRAPH OF THE CHILDREN

in the family photograph
i can match names to faces
and that is all

my eyes would drift to the youngest sister
with straight black hair
and eyes that looked beyond you
once i asked "tell me about her"
"she was smart, spoke Hebrew
and always talked of Palestine"

alone in a strange land
how many times did my grandmother enter
that picture, a playhouse
where she held her little sister
and touched the forehead of her brother

when she worked the immigrant hours
stitching days to nights
it was tucked inside her, the hope
her family would cross the sea,
where the water thinned at the channel
of her breasts and ran through her cotton dress

one brother arrived in Montreal
the others: sisters parents uncles and aunts
erased the family name
as they walked into the gas chambers

my eyes always find

the youngest child

in the lower left-hand corner

i see her separated from the others

and finally parted

from her long black hair

i wonder about her last moments, her last gasp

the mark her thin nails made

as she scraped the walls

for a hand full of air

THE SOUND TRAVELLER

under the full moon i rattle the sacred

artifacts that have passed from hand to hand

calling the voices wherever they are lodging in their lofty retreats

with a clear view of the world to join me and my silence

i give thanks to the fertility of those who carried me in the unfamiliar

sounds of rapids rushing blood the falls where tributaries married

and families merged so i would be born so i would sing this silent song

my tongue stumbles over mountains and plains

sliding backwards over consonants i hear the trapped

echo clawing its way out of Eastern European languages

the journey is of sounds, i move my feet

to the accordion, to this hill where they gathered

as a family three times a year

i evoke the names, slap the straight razor across the leather strap

so the bearded voices appear in my zeyda's shop

for their Sunday shave, i tap the tea cup with a spoon

its rose pattern, a family crest, brings the din of diners to the table

i hear the drum roll

of knife and fork on empty plates

the door from the dining room to the kitchen swinging open

in a house i never knew

my great-grandmother marches in

one hot dish after another and faraway

the creaking of a rocking chair

an unknown voice speaking

of those who lived long ago

i wander in the current of years that runs through my ears

sink in sounds of crusted snow as i come to winter

and wood cottages they called homes

so that my bones would curl into my flesh and i would be them

as they rose in the mornings with their foggy breath

as they carried water over the ice to wash

i seek the last ember of the fire that hides under the dead

a seed in the pocket of their blood

THE FIRST POGROM

it was the warnings of the rabbis and the fears of the peasants stepping out
to embrace, it was a cloud of dust, a faceless rider moving over the mountain
of the unimaginable, it was a dark hand stretching up over the village
cracking its knuckles and the bones of Jews who scattered through the market
it was a steel tongue licking blood from heart spleen and liver
the arms of fire waving on thatched roofs
to the gong of broken glass (there were no church bells)
it was wild beasts ravaging skirt and shirt
behind overturned stalls

he remembered the animals
the barn and ran holding the small hands
of younger brothers and sisters
through the corridor of screams the field of pleas
the stream of blood the last words of Mr. Averbaum dropping
the children into this dugout
this was either the best hiding place
in the village or a shallow family grave

TIMING

i marvel at my grandfather's timing
he knew when to move
while others listened
as the revolutionary steps were explained
he could hear the music
of concrete and cranes of the party
welding theories so that his brothers
would waltz inside the Russian cage

he kicked his legs over borders
became a tree in the forest
as patrols passed by
all the while humming a native tune
the orchestra pit empty in his stomach

he was light and carried himself
with what all refugees carry
sew into the lining of their clothes
or hide in secret compartments of the body–
the promise of tomorrow

he danced the night he danced through the white
ashes of field and family
two-stepped over the fallen pirouetted
around gunshots and the unforeseen
cruelty and we were there
three generations waiting in the balcony
of darkness to scream and applaud

THE MAN WITH NO PROFESSION

in a time when everyone was known by his profession
so and so the cobbler, so and so the butcher–
he was nameless
his wagon moved in the early morning
as hunters checked their traps
or in the dark of night the wheels woke
the silent village
women whispered by the well
and the men said nothing as they slipped out back
behind the woodshed or beside the barn
to retrieve what he had left
in clear bottles
they twisted the cork
and swallowed quickly
the performance was about to begin
they could feel the fuse
alive in their lungs
the cannon fired
their bodies launched
and they landed with smoking breath
giving thanks to the man
with no profession

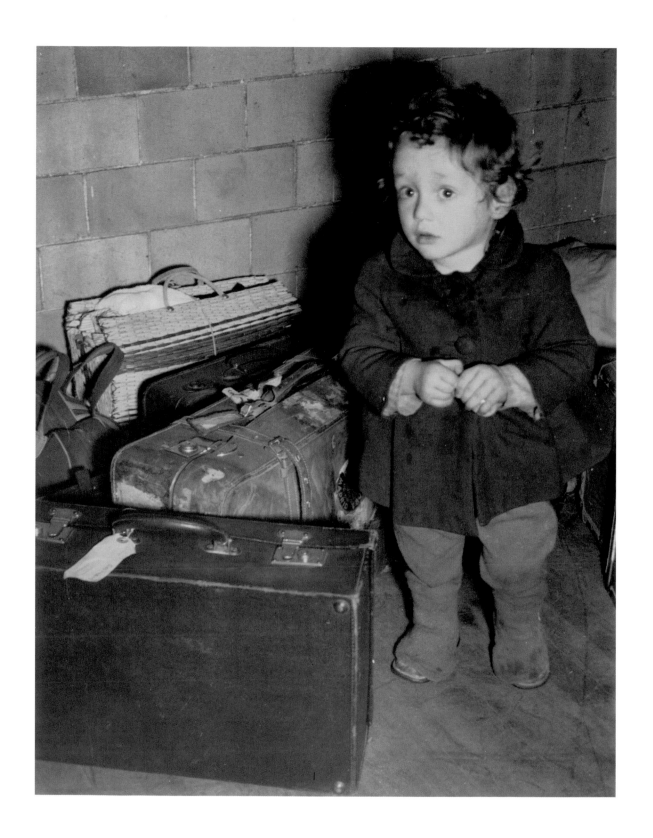

ON BEING DISCOVERED A STOWAWAY

as the canvas was lifted he could feel hundreds of silver eyes

crawling over him, the octopus arms of sailors

tying his legs and hands

a trial at sea

the black waters a judge's robes

he was sinking with the treasure of youth

locked inside his body

without a passport

or a language he could speak

swordfish swam by

on familiar ocean streets

his wig was gone

the yellow dress a lively death shroud

he was sinking into the world

he heard nothing but a solemn voice

"how long since you've eaten boy?"

MY GRANDFATHER AND THE BLUES

as the cantor holds the last high note
the performance is over
the people smile
and my grandfather
leans over to tell me
"pray putting your soul
into words not some sweet melody"

i think about his life
a village in Russia
where a member of the congregation chanted
the holy texts
shouting leaping crying
by the river that divides
this world from the next
and later at B'nai Jacob
where the cantor stood before all
his head leaning back
while his hands spoke to the L-rd

i turn away unconvinced, then i think
of the blues
how a song is (never sung
but) stomped, broken, shattered as tiny pieces
pierce the vocal chords, how notes and words are dragged
through country back roads and there is only dust
in the throat or the severing of a cord
as a spear strikes the heart

and how sometimes it is my grandfather in synagogue
rocking back and forth
on the edge of a cliff
calling out to the world with everything he's got
except his voice

MY BUBBY'S HOUSE

she began the day with the morning prayers
thanking G-d for opening her eyes
and the ritual washing of hands
that distanced her from the long journey

in darkness the body elopes with the soul
to a place across the border
where the marriage is certified
for a day or dissolved in dark mist

the traveller robbed of memories
finds himself at home
unable to dream
of architecture or cuisine
in a land so foreign

to this day when i wake
with the first sounds
of the dog barking, the alarm clock
or the light that passes over my face
i open my eyes
and look heavenward

89 CLARENCE STREET

my father and i return to his old neighbourhood
and we cross over
into the world of work horses
men in shirt sleeves, dirty aprons
a milk wagon rushes by
and one by one the neighbours appear
the fishmonger, tinsmith and grocer

we arrive at 89 Clarence Street
my father has come back to this shop
where he has pawned his memories
come back with his son
to collect everything he has left behind
come back as a pilgrim to touch sacred stones
as a tourist to view the sites
come back as the youngest child
searching for something sweet to savour

the door opens
my zeyda stands behind the glass counter
rows of work shirts and pants on shelves, boots line the floor
my bubby on the stairs, swollen blue fingers
wiping down tar paper walls, her skin clear
(she is the young woman i have met
in black and white pictures
where no one smiled) my grandfather pulls
his gold pocket watch from his vest
soon it will be time for lunch

this is how we return
floating on sweet smells
raspberries picked in the right season
fermented, breathing out loud for the first time
as the top is twisted off

my father is drawn into dusty years
squinting to see the signs
of the tailor and the five and dime
the faces of school children as they run
holding on to their caps, shoes with holes
bellies sinking lower than the stock exchange

by the school yard he turns cold
remembers the race
the shouts of the family doctor
as he arrived at the isolation ward
to the cheers of his mother
who watched and prayed
through a small window for sixty days

we wander the streets of Lower Town
my father calls on uncles Benny and Moe
who've gone to Chicago
and Henry the gentle giant
has moved on, the houses now boutiques and cafés
but the walls of memory never come down

oh let me pass this way as i move on newly paved roads
let me feel the crowds of relatives around me
touching me, one on my head, another on my back
let me carry their cardboard suitcases with thick straps
let my grip be strong
let nothing fall or break

3

BOTH SIDES

on both sides the lines are long
years you cannot see
a continuous march on the land
all in mourning
carrying their unborn
the amputated families and lovers
the memory hemorrhaging on the deeds
the will of the dead

and this is the torture
to know you have survived
to live it again
in memory, in dreams, in deeds
a prisoner of war

THE CONFLICT

in the distance black clouds
approaching, approaching as night
the earth shakes a whistle sounds
there is no time
the conductors call out: birthrights!
battle sites! holy places!

the engineers on posters and podiums
shovel fear and hatred
into the flames
faster and faster
and no one can brake this train—
one generation following another
over the borders into the sand,
the earth we so justly claim
finally claims us

AFTER THE DEATH OF CANADIAN MARNIE KIMELMAN
BY TERRORISTS ON A TEL AVIV BEACH, JULY 1990

1   the beach severed from summer
    bleeds bright
    the final breath
    seaweed on wave

2   we cannot leave her
    lying in the sand
    eyes sealed to the sun
    she calls to us
    and we return to the shore

3   the maple leaf
    wet and limp
    falls
            to the ground

4   her family
    empty
    as the chair
    empty as the future
    the memory sticks pictures
    to blank pages

KIBBUTZ SHAMIR
ON A FRIDAY AFTERNOON, JULY 17, 1981

one by one we returned to the north
first to Kiryat Shmonah
then hitchhiking the long road
past cotton fields and orchards

we stopped at the guardhouse
listened for the breeze
the last sigh
of a week about to die

on a friend's porch
we stirred old memories
watched children play
in the remaining hours of light

the sun fell gracefully
multicoloured on trees
branches meshed shadows
a safety net
between day and darkness

familiar voices and laughter
could not drown out continued rocket barrages
merely transplant them
somewhere in the night

שיר לשלום

תנו לשמש לעלות
לבוקר להאיר
זכה שבתפילות
אותנו לא תחזיר
מי אשר כבה נרו
ובעפר נטמן
בכי מר לא יעירו
לא יחזיר לכאן
איש אותנו לא ישיב
מבור תחתית אפל
כאן לא יועילו
לא שמחת הנצחון
ולא שירי הלל

פזמון חוזר:

לכן רק שירו
שיר לשלום
אל תלחשו תפילה
מוטב תשירו שיר לשלום
בצעקה גדולה.

תנו לשמש לחדור
מבעד לפרחים
אל תביטו לאחור
הניחו להולכים
שאו עיניים בתקווה
לא דרך כוונות
שירו שיר לאהבה
ולא למלחמות
אל תגידו יום יבוא
הביאו את היום
כי לא חלום הוא
ובכל הכיכרות
הריעו רק שלום.

פזמון חוזר:

תנו לשמש לעלות
לבוקר להאיר
הזקה שבתפילות
אותנו לא תחזיר
אל תגידו יום יבוא
הביאו את היום
כי לא חלום הוא
ובכל הכיכרות
הריעו רק שלום

פזמון חוזר X3 פעמים

ON THE NIGHT RABIN WAS KILLED

on the night Rabin was killed the voices of the holy
could not reach G-d, as the Song of Peace swirled into the clouds
higher and mightier, and the prayer of one man was the only prayer
that reached the celestial ear

fallen soldiers spit out mouthfuls of grave
so they could join in his song
their voices lifting his chariot
as he began the journey home

midwives ran through the country
screaming the name of birth
the bleeding had begun, a nation felt pain
peace was moving inside them
peace was about to be born

on the night Rabin was killed
the people stood still like candles
a pale fog moved across the moon
the last sacrifice was offered
to the god of war
and a thousand voices
from the concrete square
united in one flame

Opposite page: The "Song of Peace" found in the breast pocket of assassinated Israeli Prime Minister Yitzhak Rabin.

on the night Rabin was killed
four bullets flashed
illuminating the code for all holy works
talmudists found hidden tractates
mystics tallied numerical equations
and in one voice
and many languages they said
"there is no mystery
the way is clear"

on the night Rabin was killed
jugglers and fire-eaters performed
in the temples and pilgrims walked
to their homes, this too was holy
they sought the spirit
and the spirit was everywhere
on the Temple Mount, in the Old City, in the New City
in the Russian Compound, in the Armenian Quarter
in El Aksa, in Al-Quds
and in the gardens of Gethsemane

on the night Rabin was killed
the curtain was raised
and the future was clear
peace was crowned king, and the people stood
on their rooftops to watch it
parade through the streets
the masses followed the king
and the king followed his father's casket

the last song was sung
and its words, the words of peace
clung to buildings trees hearts and eyes
as he was lowered and covered over
the last missile slid into its silo
and the earth fell

                    into place

"BY THE WAY EZRA I FORGIVE YOUR ANTI-SEMITISM"
–Allen Ginsberg in a conversation with Ezra Pound

they are all seated at the great literary table

and as they move around the circle

all eyes are on Pound

who made the game fashionable

to his right Eliot

waving the original manuscript

of *The Waste Land*, and the stakes get higher

Lorca wearing his double-breasted bullet holes

tosses words on Jews of New York

their noses landing in the pile

Dylan Thomas belches, plays the ace

his own recording of Yeats's "Lament

for Mrs. Mary Moore"

and Jack Kerouac's mother

peering over his cards

whispers "the joker, the conspiracy theory"

Larkin bluffing all these years

with his poems

reveals a hand full

of personal letters

THE CHÂTEAU

leafing through the book on artists
who perished in the Holocaust
we saw our dream retreat, the château
with its poppies showcasing summer
its silent fields of visitors
tall grass waving to another time...

we sat on the grounds watching the sun reflect
on silver trays
savoured foods of a well-known chef
and cycled the country roads that wind
their way through history
like barb wire

and what of the people of Compiègne
the elderly lady who invited us in
to view her roses and the well
a thing of the past she said
like her garden soirées
for SS officers and camp guards

collaborators live in the ground
as they do on earth–
with no memory of their deeds
without hearing or seeing anything
as small and silent as a train
or its whistle leaving for Drancy
their bodies begging for a spine

i cry out to those who are missing
who never sipped champagne
waiting for the afternoon
to push its heavy light into evening
or shine on the faces of those who turned
to live their lives in darkness

when we hopped on the train
we turned around for one last look–
a station, railway lines, a small town
surrounded by smaller villages
and fields and more fields where nothing grows

DORA BARACK AT 95

we gather to listen
as she recites the last words
of a language

with every breath
she is the ghetto orchestra
perfecting the music
for its own ear
she is all the painters
who buried their works
with a prayer
and the theatre company
performing to empty chairs

she has no time—
for memorial candles
there are poems that must be written
and audiences waiting
for the words of another Yiddish poet
that will fly above the narrow streets
the ghetto the guards the gas
will circle the room
and return to the heavens

Opposite page: "The Stage" painted by Frantisek Zelenka on August 27, 1943 depicts the stage
he designed for dramatic productions in Theresienstadt, which were held in an attic.

WHEN YOU SPEAK

when you speak
about eternity
remember you're standing
on someone else's ruins

parts remain towering
a reminder to all architects
the mosaic bird
tiled into the palace floor
never flew

NOTES

Page 17	The **tombs of Absalom and Zechariah** are located in the Kidron Valley. These massive rock monuments are visible from the walls of the Old City of Jerusalem.
Page 19	A **khamsin** is a hot dry wind that may blow dust or sand.
Page 23	**Caesarea** is situated along the Mediterranean coast north of Tel Aviv. It was built by Herod the Great to resemble a typical Roman city of its day.
Page 37	**Halutzim** were those zionists who moved to Palestine and subjected themselves to severe hardship in order to make arid tracks of land fertile.
Page 59	**B'nai Jacob** was an orthodox synagogue that existed in Ottawa, Canada from 1914 to 1971.
Page 63	**Bubby** is the Yiddish word for grandmother.
Page 65	**Clarence Street** is located in the Market area of Ottawa, Canada.
Page 65	**Zeyda** is the Yiddish word for grandfather.
Page 75	**Marnie Kimelman** was born in Toronto, Canada on September 4, 1972. She was killed by a terrorist's bomb in Tel Aviv on July 28, 1990. She is survived by her parents, Harold and Linda Kimelman and brothers Jason and Marc.
Page 77	**Kibbutz Shamir** was founded in 1935 by members of the HaShomar HaZair movement from Romania. It sits on the western slopes of the northern Golan Heights and overlooks the Hula Valley.
Page 77	**Kiryat Shmonah** is a northern town in Israel that is located near the Lebanese-Israeli border.
Page 80	The **El Aksa Mosque** is the third holiest shrine in the Islamic religion after Mecca and Medina. It is located in the Old City of Jerusalem at the spot believed to be where Solomon's palace stood.
Page 80	**Al-Quds** is the Arabic name for Jerusalem.

PARTICIPATING ARTISTS

Rafi Aaron is the initiator, curator and poet of the travelling exhibit and book *A Seed In The Pocket Of Their Blood*. He was born in Ottawa, Canada and lived in Israel from 1982 to 1990. His poems have appeared in English and Hebrew translation and in such anthologies as *Vintage 96* (Quarry Press), 1996 and *More Garden Varieties Two* (Mercury Press), 1990. He received The Tel Aviv Foundation writer's grant for his collection of poetry *The Lost And Found* (Amphitheatre Publications Ltd.), 1990. In 1996 his poem "This Is The Child" won third prize in the League of Canadian Poets annual competition. His 1990 reading tour of the United States was organized by P.E.N. Israel and the Cultural Department of the Foreign Ministry of Israel. Rafi Aaron lives in Toronto, Canada.

Karolina Barski was born in Edmonton, Canada in 1980. She currently lives in Vancouver and attends Point Grey Secondary School. One of her photographs was selected by Kodak for the travelling exhibit *Images Of Who We Are*, Toronto, Montreal, and Vancouver, 1996.

Werner Braun has been a photographer in Israel for over fifty years. He has eighteen books to his credit and has worked in a wide range of areas, from photo-journalism to landscape photography.

Serge Clément photographs have appeared in exhibits, books, private collections and museums in Canada and abroad. Among his many solo exhibitions are: *Four Days In The life Of Quebec*, Art Gallery of Ontario, 1996 and *Cité Fragile*, Mois de la Photo, Paris, 1994. His publications include *Cité Fragile* (Vox Populi), 1992 introduction: Christian Caujolle; text: François Jalbert.

Linda Dawn Hammond lives in Toronto, Canada and specializes in portrait photography and digital montage. Her work has appeared in books, newspapers and magazines throughout North America. She received her Master of Fine Art from York University in 1996.

Eran Harduf currently resides in Rome, Italy and is a photography graduate from The Canadian Hadassah-Wizo Neri Bloomfield College in Israel. His areas of specialty are commercial photography and social documentation. His work has been displayed in numerous group shows in Israel.

Jim Hollander was born in the United States and is the chief photographer for Reuters in Israel. His photography exhibit *Art Of The Caves*, Art Gallery of Ontario Extension Services, 1977, travelled throughout Ontario.

Doron Horowitz lives in Haifa, Israel. Since 1988 he has been the chief photographer for the Nature Reserves Authority of Israel and *Eretz Magazine*. His photographs have appeared in geographic magazines in Israel, Japan, Europe and the United States.

Gaye Jackson lives in Toronto, Canada and is a member of the Tenth Muse Studio, a colletive of artists producing photo-based work. Currently she has work touring in the group show *Persistent Documents,* which opened at Le Mois de la Photo, Montreal, 1995.

Ruth Kaplan lives in Toronto, Canada and specializes in portrait photography. Her photographs have appeared in major Canadian publications and brought her numerous National Magazine Awards. She has received grants from the Canada Council, the Ontario Arts Council and the Toronto Arts Council.

Shimon Lev is a landscape photographer who lives in Jaffa, Israel. He is a regular contributor to *Eretz Magazine* and *Hamasa Achar* as well as numerous journals and magazines outside of Israel. His book *Das Land Der Bible* (Gratz), 1995 was a compilation with Wolfgang Sotill. His one man show *Active Souls* was displayed at The Gallery at the College of Design in Haifa in 1995.

David Rubinger lives in Jerusalem, Israel and began working for *Time Magazine* in 1954. Since then he has covered almost every historic event in the Middle East for *Time/Life*. The publication of his book *Witness To An Era (Time/Life)*, 1988 coincided with Israel's 40th anniversary celebrations. His permanent photography exhibit is on view in the International Convention Centre in Jerusalem.

Natalie Schonfeld lives in Toronto, Canada and graduated from Ryerson Polytechnic University in 1997 in photographic arts. Her first solo exhibit was *Life is Else(where?)*, 8 Elm Gallery, Toronto, 1995. Her work was featured in *Beyond Belief*, Ryerson Gallery, Toronto, 1997. Her area of specialization is social documentation.

Frantisek Zelenka was a famous stage designer who was born in Kutna Hora, Czechoslovakia. While interned in Theresienstadt for two years he designed the sets and costumes for the dramatic productions that were performed in a squalid attic by internees. In 1944 he was deported to Auschwitz where he perished.

Special thanks to the Canadian Jewish Congress National Archives, the Ghetto Fighters House (Beit Lohamei Hagetaot) Israel, the Nature Reserves Authority of Israel, Kibbutz Shamir Archives and the City of Ottawa Archives for allowing the author to reproduce photographs from their collections in this book. Thanks to Eretz Magazine for assisting the author to locate landscape photographers in Israel, and the Ottawa Jewish Historical Society for giving the author access to their archive material.

Photograph Credits

Doron Horowitz	14, 34, 90
Werner Braun	16, 24
Shimon Lev	18, 22, 74
Eran Harduf	28, 76
Jim Hollander	30
Kibbutz Shamir Archives	36
Courtesy of Benjamin Feinstein	42
Natalie Schonfeld	46
Serge Clément	50, 54, 62, 72
Karolina Barski	52
Canadian Jewish Congress Archives	56, 82
Ruth Kaplan	58
City of Ottawa Archives	64
David Rubinger	78
Gaye Jackson	84
Ghetto Fighters House, Israel	88
Nature Reserves Authority of Israel	90